MW01248488

In the Body of a Mind

In the Body of a Mind

Kayla Estelle Elfers

LIGHTNING TOWER PRESS

In the Body of a Mind by Kayla Estelle Elfers

Published by Lightning Tower Press, LLC
P.O. Box 381
Shoreham, NY 11786

Copyright © 2023 by Kayla Estelle Elfers

All rights reserved. No portion of this book may be reproduced in any form without written permission from the publisher, except as permitted by U.S. copyright law. For permissions, address Lightning Tower Press, LLC., P.O. Box 381, Shoreham, NY 11786
lightningtowerpress@gmail.com

Characters and places in this book are either a product of the author's imagination or used fictitiously. Any resemblance to persons alive or dead is coincidental. Descriptions of harm and violence are used creatively at the author's discretion.

This book is set in 11-point Garamond.

Library of Congress Control Number:
2023944729

ISBN 979-8-9865558-0-5 (Print)
ISBN 979-8-9865558-1-2 (Ebook)

Printed in the United States of America.

First Edition: 2023

5 4 3 2

I dedicate my first published book to my Papa and my Mom. These two were the first people to listen to me read in front of an audience, and they are always rooting for me. Not to mention they are two of my favorite people in the whole wide world.

Thank you, my first and biggest supporters.

Anatomy

Up and down, up and down, up and down. There's a roller coaster rummaging behind my bedroom door. My buckle is strapped tightly to my gut. Though I am ready to ride the roller coaster each day, the major jerks and downhill jolts only happen in the privacy behind my bedroom door. Each time the roller coaster goes up. It goes through the window and up to the sky for all to see. My neighbors can see my smile glistening in the sun as I scream with such happiness and gratitude that I get to experience this ride, right here and right now. I wave to my parents as the roller coaster swirls me in the air like a leaf blowing in the wind. When I go up in the roller coaster I am so close to the sun that I become sunshine. I love being up. And then that's when the roller coaster tips and treks down, smashing into my house and slamming my bedroom door shut. It spins in a small circle over and over. My blinds aren't open and there's no sunlight anymore. My smile fractures to a frown while I grip the handles in front of me.

Cerebral Cortex

The Interrogation Room[1]

I sit
On the
Grey faux
Leather chair
In the Interrogation
Room with the
Silent and still-
Learning Rookie
To my left
And the Blunt
Assertive Older Man
In front of me.
Bright and warm
Fluorescent lights
Shine on me.
I don't sweat
Or show any
Signs of fear.
I smile.

Mom told me
To be honest.

The first few questions
(The courteous but disposable
Questions used to ease
Into a more intense conversation),
I was.

And then Rookie typed
Away on a pristine
Computer — no idea what
Was written but I know
How it made me feel.

"A patient etherized upon a table."

Older Man asks me why
I am here in a
Professional tone.
Do I tell Older Man Everything?
Do I be honest?
Courage.
But I've been
Honest before.
Look where it
Got me.
In a cyclical
State of being.

"In the room women come and go
Talking of Michaelangelo."

The blonde hairs on
My twig arms rise.

I go quiet.

"And indeed there will be time."

I speak
But not the
Truth.

Rookie click clacks keys
Typing so swiftly
But all I can focus on is
Older Man and how his
Face wanes into a small
Suppression of his brows.

Older Man knew why I came
Yet I couldn't acknowledge it.

Couldn't even say it.

"So how should I presume?"

I spit up a sly sentence,

He cups it into his hands.
The smallest bit of detail.
Older Man talks to Rookie in
Their unrecognizable lab jargon.
Rookie clacks away again
While Older Man grabs
The needle and the band.

He asks me, "Which arm?"
I say, "I don't care, whichever is easiest."
He says, "It's your arm, not mine."

So I choose the one with less scars,
The more natural arm.

He asks me, "Would you feel more
Comfortable lying down?"
I say, "If it's easier for you, sure."
He says, "You're the patient."

I sit straight up with a
Slight sag in my shoulders.
I feel the band go around my arm.
Older Man asks me to make a fist.
My three attempts were laughable.
He wiggles the needle into my inner arm.

For a split second I imagine the image
Of this moment, a heroin addict trying to get high.
I'm not a heroin addict but my
Lack of honesty about my harmful addiction

Is the reason why my blood is being tested.

I leave.

"This is not what I meant, at all."

And I, like Prufrock
Resonate as the Fool.

Cerebellum

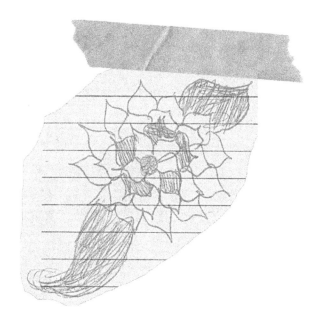

The Walk

I five look'd at you with my widened eyes.
How do you still make time for your daughter?
You smiled even when I made up lies.
Your high hopes for me now in the slaughter.

"Are you disappointed with your child?"
I asked but you smile and shake your head.
No matter what, you walk me to the aisle:
I accomplish? Or fail to see ahead?

I hugged you at five each morning, each day.
I hold your arm tight on my wedding day.

A Basic Conversation

Am I?
But I didn't mean that.
Can you just say it one more time?
Don't make me.
Entitled, right?
Fuck, not what I meant.
Gosh, no need for harsh language.
How was I supposed to not get mad?
I don't know but why call me that?
Just quit it, please.
Kind. I am a kind person.
LOL sure, okay.
Maybe you don't think so, but I am.
Not all of the time.
Oh, so you think I'm entitled AND a bad person?
Please stop! I never said that.
Question, you're implying that though, right?
Really? We're gonna do this . . . again?
Seriously, you mean it, don't you?
Tell me you're joking.
Understand that I am—
—Very, very rich because of Daddy.
Wait let me finish.
Xenas, I don't care how rich you are, I love you.
You love me?
Zealously (even if you're entitled and a tad dramatic)

Is Earl Home?

WELCOME HOME!
        Home.
                Is Earl home?
        He's sick, sweating with a sweater on.
                He's still coping with change.
It's not a home.
        It's no home.
                But it is a house.
It is *the* house.
        Earl's heart — fluttery with all that he now sees
                In this trippy, abandoned house that he
Is *not* living in.
                No.
        Earl brings his breath to further escalate the situation.
                . . . Or so I thought. I told him to leave the house.
                I never told him to leave home.
                I refuse to listen to him again.
        His positive outlook on life.
(It's morbid)
        His positivity is a beat on its own.
        This beat should not have been used this way.

        Memories, highlights.
        Earl makes an interesting echo.
Not beat.
Not home.
Just the house
                Earl left me in. Is he home?

Piccola Ragazza

Piccola Ragazza
Steps on lumps of
Pesce.
Her family of
Pesci si transforma into clear dolphins. They
Verso il sole.
Little Girl
Saluta e una sola
Tear sheds into
Nell'oceano.

Confessions

Volatility viciously
Eviscerates the organ
Of fuel and fulfillment.

My mirror.
My phone.
My culture.

I can't control the cacophony
In my meek mind that
Makes me pull a trigger and
Lets my guts spew like garbage
Into a bowl of hidden secrets.

My mirror.
My phone.
My culture.

Battling body and mind
~~I've strengthened my self image~~
By knowing my ~~self~~ worth.

Wishes and wants ~~worthy~~
Of a body beautiful ~~as is~~
And ~~worthy~~ of a life lived
With less pain personally
Inflicted.

Finally falling ~~in love~~
With ~~who I am and~~
The person I am becoming.

Struggling ~~sometimes~~ to stop
Myself.

But ~~less~~ transactions have
Been made between me
And my demons

Once I spotted the light
~~That shines within myself.~~

Unwritten

I
Once
Overcame
Destiny
With a pen
In my
hand.

Why Do You Look Sad?

WaHaHa! I'm not sad! WaHaHa.
      Yeah but you're crying.
WaHaHaHa!
      Oh, don't be sad, Kay. Just smile.
WaHaHaHaHa! I don't want to.
      What's going on, Kay?
WaHaHaHaHaHa! Everything and anything.
      Kay, don't overexaggerate.
WaHaHaHaHaHaHa! But I'm not.
      You're always unhappy and you barely eat.
WaHaHaHaHaHaHaHa! Does this mean I'm finally skinny?
      What's wrong with you? You always know how to ruin my
      day.
WaHaHaHaHaHaHaHaHaHa!
      What's wrong with you?
WaHaHaHaHaHaHaHaHaHaHa! Everything and anything.
      You have a great life, you should be grateful for it.
WaHaHaHaHaHaHaHaHaHaHaHa! I am. I'm just sad.
wahaha.

Occipital

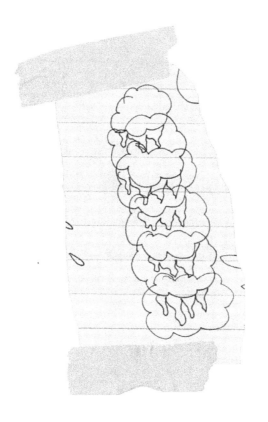

Still

Gutted sand out of the hourglass.
Stunted growth on the arm's pass.

The clock locked in its place
Frozen left to erase
What mattered in the space.

The sun doesn't rise
The way it used to climb
The sky with no sense of time
Falling down the depths of its demise.

How the clock used to wrap itself
With its arms on the twelfth
Now they're spreaded lines on a round shelf.

How the hourglass filled with grains
Leaving its top with no remains
Now what's left in the bottom drains.

Two separate entities, two halves of a whole.
(Can past and future intertwine
When present is undermined?)
A shoe pulled apart from its sole.
Speeding hurts and takes a toll.

Toys Made for the Girl and Boy That Play[2]

To tinker tin toys takes time.
Building bountiful boundaries.
Timeless takes twice time to tinker.
How has his, hers come to this?

Relationship rebuilt like toys—
Plastic and chintzy, wobbling to
Craft two tin toys to stand
Equidistant and balanced.
To think these two toys
Stood on their own.

Now
Their relationship relies relentlessly
On their codependence, falling
Foolishly to the floor, unable
To stand rebuilt because,
To tinker tin toys takes time
But rebuilding boundaries barricades
Improvements that could never last.

Distant Relative

She put the telephone down
Instantly biting her already-chewed-up nails.

Her eyes bouncing back and forth
from the phone to the letter like a tennis match.

Suddenly a single tear falls from her milky eyes.

She's paralyzed in time.

She reads the letter one more time,
This time.

She understands no one will pick up the phone
At home anymore.

Bones on Cement

Raggedy, rigid bones lay upon cement,
Chained to the bricks that could
Cut through skin.
No heat.
But no flesh.
All that's left are the bones
That can't be sliced and
Can't feel the cold.
They're used to punishment.
I'm sure the prisoner
Dealt with punishments, too.
Maybe they didn't last
Through the chains, cements, and bricks.
Maybe they gave up.

But their bones are still present.

Hollow Hand

I'm breathing
Down
The back of his neck,
Hoping
He remembers how
To give a peck.

Slobber glossing
Over
His cruel intention.
My
Mind's left in
Another dimension.

My body is
Hollow
Beside him,
Hand
No longer a
Loving limb.

Extended my arm but it
Snapped.
Yet he's walking ahead left
Untapped.

Not Erased

His hands smooth—
Fingers gliding
On paper
As he leaves
Lead marks
In gradients
And shapes and lines.
Consistent techniques
Until a jagged mark
Abrupts his piece.
He scavenges
For the perfect
Square to abort
The unwanted dot on
His creation.
He never used the
Square, did he even
Own it?
He leaves
But the mark stays.

The Story of Water and Fire

The story of
Water and fire
Goes like this:
False friends
Finding the underlying meaning
To their bond.
Water so calm and soothing
Maintaining a balance between
Fire, so active and disruptive.
A friendship doomed from the
Start.

Water cooled and suppressed the
Anger within Fire.
Fire burned for Water's act of kindness.
Fire yearned for Water
But Water was just ebbing and flowing
Like Water does.

Fire, burning mad, forced
Their flames on to
Water in hopes Water
Would feel an ounce
Of the flaming passion
Fire feels.

Water never wanted
Anything more than
To ebb and flow
Alongside Fire.
Water never wanted
To find themselves
Tarnishing the flames
That attacked Water

So peacefully, so passionately.

Fire's flames died, soaked and misted
By Water.
Fire fled to the desert,
Far away from the chaos and rejection of water.

Water stayed.
Processing and raining
And storming and making
Waves larger than Water ever
Thought was possible.

Water became a force
Of feared immensity,
Something only Fire
Gawks about in the dry
Distance.

Water can't see Fire anymore
Like Fire can see Water.
But Water can puncture holes
Into Fire's actions,
Drowning flames with swift, fluid movement.

Every time Fire lights flames,
Water smothers these bickering nuisances
And forges a new narrative

Without Fire.

Backyard

Have you ever been captivated
By mundane beauty?

Walked outside and melted
In the sweet stinging warmth of
The sun.

It's quiet until you listen to the
Birds' subtle chirps and the trees'
Timid rustle.

How is it that such a normal
Backyard can transform itself into
Such a tropical treasure?

A rainforest made of sunlight,
Grass, dew, and your dog
Running around the driest
Patches of dirt.

The wind kisses your face so
Gently, calmly bringing the empty
Beer cans to life with
Harmonious and hollowed out whistles

Somehow this place is magic.
Solitude surrenders the self,
Releasing all rigid emotions that used to be bottled up in glasses
And now here you are.
Once filled with saddened substances
Now drained of the disconsolate contents to
Be filled with the shimmery sunlight that is peace.

B&C Thoughts of 1933

After January fifth,
She rides shotgun.
Long hair pinned back.
A gun tangled in between her
hands. He takes her to the bank.
She wants to open the car door.
But there are consequences to flying.
She clings to her seat. She's now used to
The thrills of riding with him.
She romanticizes veering off the road
And riding to a home of their own,
Where she holds no guns, just a ring.

Before May twenty-third,
He drives west.
Hair hidden by his hat.
She adjusts it to sit properly
On his head.
She takes him places he never
Thought he'd see in his lifetime.
He wants to love her.
But there are consequences to flying.
He sits back in his seat. He soon
Reminisces the thrills of driving with her.
He romanticizes a wealthy life with her
And no hats to hide partial identities.

Below the Bell

It's like that one
Carnival game where
The man must pound
Down a fake hammer
To make a ball hit
The top of a bell.

We hold men to a
Standard
And sometimes they
Hit the bell on
The first try.
But when we
Bring back the bell
To be hit
They cannot carry
The weight
Of the ax,
Nor the swinging
Motions meant to
Entertain us
And reassure us
That they
Are putting in effort.

The roller coaster jerks me to the left and I suddenly feel like I can't handle being on the roller coaster anymore. I can't see what surrounds me even though I am in my room. It's so dark. I take my hands off the handles and claw at my wrists, my thighs, my whole body. I want to feel something other than fear. I suddenly feel warmth from my wrists and my thighs. I created sunshine for myself. The roller coaster slows down. I can't seem to remember how I created sunshine in the dark, all I know is that I slowed down the roller coaster because I made sunshine in the dark. I wipe a straggling tear from my chin and suddenly the roller coaster goes out the window towards the sun. The moment my eyes adjust to the radiance I can see the sunshine I made in the dark. Now that I am in the sun again, I can see that I did not make sunshine in the dark. I made something else. I realize now that the roller coaster has me outside, anyone can see the stains and marks on my wrists and my thighs. I quickly fold my arms in my lap. I can no longer hold onto the handles in front of me. I don't want anyone to see what I created. I sit uncomfortably still in my seat as the roller coaster takes me closer to the sun. The warmth of the sun feels refreshing as it dries my once-wet face. My smile reappears. For a moment it's quiet. I look around and there's no one watching me. I lean back and extend my arms towards the sun. I am sunshine until my wrists and my thighs burn pink. I tuck my arms back into my lap and hunch over. The sun doesn't like my attempt at sunshine.

Parietal

01/01/22

The first day of 2022. This year is gonna be
So much fun, I just know it.

ENTRY:
"I lost my journal, so in the meantime,
I'll state here that 2021 has
Given me so much and I look forward
To what 2022 has to offer. For me."

Blue starlight
Maximizes the sky
And I feel like Rainbow Brite.

Baseball

He walked into my life
With a slight nudge,
A small gesture
Of friendliness
Being offered
To me. Why?
I had no idea.

He wrapped my mind in
Subtle soft sounds,
Empirical evidence
Of euphonic music
Made to mimic
Euphoric feelings
Intertwining each
Thought, each
Spoken word, each
Interaction that was
And maybe still even is?

Such a shame
That we never
Played a baseball
Game. Or maybe
We never finished
What I thought we
Started.

But I want to.
I want our stadium
Lit and endless lines
Of field.
I want to be pitcher
And I want him to be
My catcher. But he isn't.

He is the batter.
We make contact,
We deceive each other.
I throw.
He hits.
He runs.
He leaves me.
A batter is never interested
In the sweetness of tangible
Back and forth throws.
A batter likes velocity,
Being chased.

Kiss Me Again and Again

Bite my bottom lip until
My blood pours from the sky.
Hold me like an injured bird.
Open your eyes, breathe. See the
Sun and moon.
Close your eyes, in sync with mine,
Envision the dark night sky
Surrounding us as we collide
Our noses and realign our lips.

Kiss me again and again.
Root yourself in me like the
Trees you plant.
Pull away and smile with me
Like a sunflower blooming in sunlight.

Kiss me again and again.
Make up for lost time as if
There's no such thing as time.
Hold my hand and kiss
My neck until the harmonies
Of the bees slowly quiet.
Stay with me until we see the
Dark night sky with our
Eyes open.
Be with me.
Be a part of my Earth.
And as always,
Kiss me again and again.

LUST

L (untamed hair top of a glistening frame)

U (enchanting eyes — bulbs of fireflies)

S (hot magnets moving toward each other)

T (a shift instilled in one another)

09/17/22

My mind is in my heart
Heart beat goes miles per minute
Beat
Beat
Beat beat

My heart isn't in my mind
Anymore
Just the thoughts of what
Could have been
Could have been
Could have been

.

Every thought is said in my inner
Monologue
Unable to stop
My voice keeps
Going and going and going and going
With no end

My eyes are glued to the black
Skies my lids provide a shield of
The inescapable world I dissolve myself.

Cuts

Skin sits smoothly
On top of muscle
Layered before bone.

Like a dagger
I cut into you.

I make contact
With flesh
Until I pierce
Muscle with
My bones.

Wounded and warm.
I evaluate my execution
Longing to cut into you
again.

Your Bike

I learned
To ride your bike
At twenty-one.
Because of you.
You taught me
How to sit upon
The saddle;
How to slowly pedal;
How to hold a
Firm grip on the arms of
Your bike.
Your bike.
I steer onto
Smooth, velvet
Down to the most
Beautiful scenery.
I move slow but
Take in all the pleasure
That comes with riding
Your bike.
Your bike gives me
A freedom I never
Knew I had.
I don't want to walk alone
Or drive alone anymore.
I only want to ride your bike.

The Doors

Bust open
When not
Expected.
Slam shut
When not
Wanted.
Why do you
Do this?
My life
Is not
Something
You can
Just walk
In and
Out of.
You can't
Shut me
Out and
Expect me
To come
Back to
You when
You turn
The knob
And enter.
Never asked
You to
Re-enter.
Never asked
You to
Leave.
But each
Time you
Leave and

Every time
You come back,
I know
I'm worth
So much
More than
The way
You treat
Me. Like doors.

No Lines

I slept in a caged box,
Confined to the lines on
The loose leaf that burned
So easily when met with your vexed child.

I've allowed myself to become one
With the liminal spaces between
Each parallel line.
I find comfort in simplicity,
But of course, your eager child
Scribbled all over my home.
He showered my safe haven
With abrupt yellows and violent blues.
He tried to become Van Gogh.

Just like that he took over
The page that was never his.

I am no longer confined to the
Spaces in between the parallel lines.
I have nowhere to go on the
Loose leaf, as he filled it with
His impish narrative.
He kicked me out of my own home.

Instead of putting him in time out,
I silently move
My pen to a blank sheet
That hasn't been claimed by him
Or me or anyone.
I never thought I'd be kicked out—
I have so much freedom.
I have a new start.

I live in an effervescent sky
Where my words no longer make space for the paper.
The paper makes space for my words.

Entry, Last

You are a story I have
Yet to finish.
You were perfectly scripted
In my book.

Until I came to the
Denouement in which
You're not a reality, mere
Fiction, falsified by the
Hopelessness of my aching
Aura.

I wish all my poems were
Memoirs but then, would
I feel so deeply anymore?
How could I ever capture
The way your eyes lock with mine
Through any other form of story,
Telling?

You may be fiction,
But you're still the
Greatest story I
Have told so far
And have yet to finish.

Let me freewrite
As much as I feel
For you and see
A plot unfold into
Our reality.

You're the story
I can never put down.

You're the story I
Always go back to.

The roller coaster treks backwards. My neighbors wave to me but I can't wave back because they might see the sunshine I tried to make for myself. So I smile at them. A forced, slightly crooked, closed smile. Once the roller coaster busts into my house I let my forced smile turn to a frown. My parents ask me what's wrong but the roller coaster is going faster, it's already in my room, slamming my bedroom door behind it. As the roller coaster spirals in the darkness, it goes even faster. I'm ashamed of this roller coaster that I am on. I can't make it stop, there's no eject button. I can slow it down. The only way I know how to be still is when I am sunshine. But there's no sunlight in my room. I panic.

Temporal

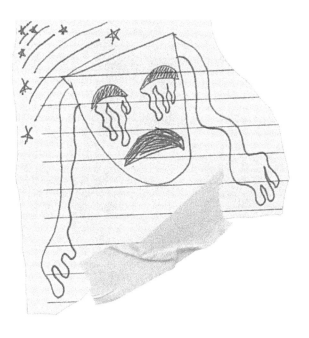

The Grandkids' Annual Visit

We tumbled down the hill.
We laughed and then got up. We
played ring-around-the-rosie. We
laughed and then got up. My
brother grabs your flowers, I
collect water from the faucet. We
make our way to you.
We plant the flowers
Right on your soil.
We look at your Cross and tell you
He's now four years old
And I am almost eight.
Joey's really good at Soccer.
And I am still dancing___.
Goodbye, we love you.

We watched them
Tumble down the hill.
They laughed and then got up. We
all played ring-around-the-rosie. We
all laughed and then got up. She
grabs your flowers,
Joey collects the water.
We all make our way to you.
We all plant the flowers
Right on your soil.
We look at your Cross and tell you
Laci is four years old and beautiful.
John is the little one in my arms.
You remember Joey, he's ten or
Maybe eleven, I forget. As for me,
I am thirteen.
And I am still dancing___.
Goodbye, we all love you.

We watched the two youngest ones
Tumble down the hill.
They all laughed and then got up.
We all played ring-around-the-rosie.
We all laughed and then got up.
John grabs your flowers.
Laci collects water from the faucet.
We all make our way to you.
We all plant the flowers
Right on your soil.
We all look at your Cross and tell you
Jaxson just turned four and he's funny for a little guy.
John is now ten and suffers from middle child syndrome.
Laci is now thirteen and wears braces and bras.
Joey is now eighteen and goes to college.
And I am still dancing through life.
Every day. For me, for them, for you.
Goodbye, we love you.

Lizard[3]

King of
Rock and Roll
Opens
The doors.
You stare into my eyes,
Looking for my soul.
Finding ways to
Break on Through.
You perceive me,
Entrancing me
With your words
Of depth and honesty.
You Love (m)Her Madly.
That's what I hear.
To my demise,
I realize I
Can no longer
Sympathize for
A king so slimy—
Lies in each
Sentence sent.
I will
Tell All the People
How I let
Your lies
Slime over my
Eyes and
Touch Me
So deeply.
With all I know
I didn't want it
To be true.
But at
The End of the Night
I was in love with

The idea of you,
A king.
I was wrong.
And as I long
For you to
Speak words
Of truth,
I know
You're a
Lizard.
Blood cold,
Heart tiny,
And brain small.
A king? You could
Never measure
To such a
Noble title.
May I humble
You with my
Blunt jargon,
As this is not
Conversation
Of mere
Passion
But one of
Transaction.
You thought
I'd give you
What you
Desired but
I'm tired.
I don't want you to
Light My Fire.
I don't need
To give in to
A game I
Never wanted
To play.

Foolish sir,
I'm no
L.A. Woman
And you are no king.
Go back to your
Hyacinth House
And say, "
Hello, I Love You
" to the
Queen of the Highway.
Do it
When the Music's Over
And the
Unknown Soldier
Appears. Maybe then
Will you rethink
Your poetic status
And realize
We Could (Never) Be So Good Together.
Go on with your life
And accept I sealed
The Doors
Shut.

Portal

The sky perfectly
Places its tears
On my windowsill.
I think, do I look this
Beautiful when I cry?
The sound of her whimpers
Are the playful euphonics,
Ringing in my ears of clairaudience.
The fascinating and sudden transformation
From bright yellow to dull green. My
Backyard is a magical forest. My mind is an imaginative
Field where my inner child is
Filled with endless questions and
Wonder.
All this amazement.
All this fascination.
Just from looking out my window.

Light My Love

You walked me
To a river
Where the water
Was a stream
Of yellows and
Tints of blues
And specs of reds.
I'd never seen
Such a stream
Of colors in the
Water.
I always thought
Rivers were blue,
And then I met you.

"Your mind is a stream of colors, extending beyond our sky."[4]

Crack / head

They called him
Crack head
Cause he
Smoked crack
Through pipes
And spoons
With his
Poor-folk
Friends. He
Robbed his own
Family
Took Mom's
Jewelry
Dad's watch
Our CDs

He ran
He went
Away
From us

He was
Always
Away
From us

Sober man
Held by
Forces
That know
Our last name
They let him
Leave. He
Comes back

Sorry
He's good
Until
He can't
Get hired
Anywhere

He goes
Back to
His friends
Takes the
Edge off
With help
Of rocks
And pipes

He's lost
Again.

Hazy
He holds
A gun
Made of
Plastic
Which he
Took from
His four
Year old
Son. He
Enters
The gas
Station
Without
Hesitation

And just
Like that
Labeled

As the
Crackhead
Junkie
Robber
Criminal.

They don't
Background
Check how
To say
His last
Name but
They do
Background
Check old
Mugshots
Of him.
We are
Grateful
They can't
Pronounce
Our last
Name so
No one
Will think
To call
Us and
Ask if
We know
Crackhead
His face
Droops in
The shot
It's drawn
Like all
Of our
Faces
We hope

No one
Will see
Resemblance
That no
One will
Know he's
Related
To us
As my
Mom's
Brother
As my
Papa's
Son
As my
Cousin's
Father
As my uncle

Only
If these
People
Knew him
Like we
Did. They'd
Hold off
But they
Keep this
News of
Crackhead
Junkie
Robber
Criminal
Beaten in
Voices
That will
Never
Care or

Know who
This man
Is
Beyond
The many
Labels
They throw
At him.
To think
They will
Never see
Memories
Of him
Throwing
Me in
The air
At my
Papa's house
Fifteen
Years ago
Memories
I know
Are tucked
Away
In the
Back of
My mind
And tucked
Somewhere
In a
Basement
Somewhere
On video
Maybe
If we're
Lucky
We'll find
Those old

Videos
And share
Those with
The news.
But they
Still won't
See how
He went
To church
Alone
Every Sunday
Confessing
His sins
Believing
In hope
And light
To guide
Him on
His path

He's my
Brother's
godfather
And that
We have
Somewhere
On video

My uncle
Made the
Best pizza
He was
A talented chef.
He wanted
To work
In his
Own place
Some day.

We have
His hopes
And dreams
Somewhere
On video

My uncle
Played sports
In his
Childhood
Hockey
Was his
Favorite
He smacked
Pucks and
Rolled through
Driveways
With a
Stick in
His hand
A smile
So wide
It could
Be deemed
Infectious
To all
That see
We have
His smile
Somewhere
On video

But these
Don't mean
A thing
To the
Reporters
So stunned by

Limelight
They'll do
Whatever
It takes
To have
Their five
Minutes
Of fame,
Where they
Tell a
Story
That they
Know nothing
About and
Isn't their
Own to tell.
Vicious
They run
Rampant
Showing
Someone's
Worst fears
Plastered in
Front of
Cameras.
Standing
In crime
Scenes like
It's an
Honor to
Announce
Someone
Screwed up
But they'll
Never
Say how
Someone
Is screwed up

And is
In need
Of help.
They gloss
Over his
Disease
Like it
Does not
Have to
Do with
What he's
Done. They
Don't care.
They don't
Care who
Is left
Hurt
Offended
Embarrassed
Traumatized.
They like
Humiliating
People and
Make a
Steady
Income
While they
Appear
On our
TV with
My uncle's
Face on
A zoomed
In screen

Crackhead
Junkie
Robber

Criminal
On television
For the
World to watch.

Hungry

"I'm sorry if I let you down"
Does that apology fill your ego?

Ooo how about:
"I'm sorry this is how it turned out"
Or "Sorry I don't like you"
Or "I'm sorry we don't talk"

It isn't my fault
But I'll take the blame.

You're angry still.
Your ego has a hunger pain.

May I remind you that
I told you platonic
And you ignored what I said
You were fixated on romantic
And forced illusions in your head.
You should've listened to what I had
To say.
But your ego is famished.

Stay starving and stay away.

To disappear[5]

To disappear

Apparition
O, mighty apparition
How doth thyself
Hold such an
Illusion on the mere
Macbeth? That he,

A man of honor,

Will burn in
The depths of greed
(With his monstrous wife)?

To disappear.
To disappear.

Witches 1,2,3
That barely can see

Beyond the misery that lies ahead,

What brings upon your premises?

Who told you this knowledge?

To disappear.
To disappear.

She Is the Wave

It's the wave
The tadpoles race the
Tiny girl's feet;
No ankle bracelets or
Toe rings or polish. Just
Purely living limbs on
A beautiful little girl. She
Smiles. She
Is the wave.

It's the wave
The frogs leap away from the
Uncollected college girl's hand;
With a tiny heart tattoo on the
Back of the wrist, and a ring on
Each finger, and polish on
Long acrylic nails. Just
A few changes on the
Limb of a woman.

It's the calm wave
The tiny girl looks at her
Reflection in immensity;
Fascinated by her
Own unique beauty, blending into
A transparent blue-green film where she
Can see her
Toes grapple the
Small grains of sand. She
Spots the tadpoles in the
Water and runs with
Them, not to them. It's
All so blissful. She
Is blissful.

It's the crashing wave
The woman stares at
Her own frown and
Furrowed brow in
The murky water;
Hovering above it,
Leaning over to
See something other than
Her face;
Only intrigued by the
Frog. She's fixated only on
      (   )
Holding the frog, she forgets how she
Looks. She
Doesn't creep up behind the
Frog, instead, she
Reaches out her
Hand to
Him. He hops away and
--
She retracts her arm. It's
A little disappointing. She's a
Little disappointing. But
Her hand folding back to herself;
Creating stunning ripples—
Ricocheting through all of the
immensity. Her acrylic nails feel the
Soft waves, kissing her finger tips in
(   )
The most gentle manner. She
Smiles. She
Is the wave.

An Actress Dancing

The young girl pulls back her hair
As the lights change from
Warm bright light to
Fluorescent pinks and blues
Changing with each new beat in
Her anthem of comfort that plays
In the tender space of her head
While she moves her body
In rhythm to her internal music

This roller coaster needs to stop and it won't, it'll keep going and going, no matter the direction I want it to go. It never stops. I close my eyes and sit back. No one can see my wrists or my thighs or my whole body. No one can see anything in my room, including myself. So why not make my own sunshine in the dark? Maybe if I try to make it once more these feelings will go away, maybe the roller coaster will finally stop. So I claw at myself. My worries fade to my nails and embed themselves into the surface of my skin, and suddenly with drips of warmth, they vanish. They go away. The roller coaster slows down again and I feel better. The roller coaster goes through the window and towards the sun. I can see the red everywhere on my body, "out damn'd spot"[6] I say as I rub my hands over and over until the red remnants are gone, but they don't disappear. The sun disappears. The sky turns gray as the roller coaster heads towards the dark clouds. My neighbors see me and wave before they go inside their homes. I wave back and they see my wrist. Before they can even ask what happened to my arm, the sky downpours. I let the cold drops of rain clean my skin. Though the red stains of warmth trickle away, I am left with marks that won't disappear. I tried to make sunshine but all I did was create more darkness for myself.

Amygdala

College Counseling

So today I went to counseling which I haven't gone to in four
years.
I went to see a counselor through the school
And they are very nice!
At the end of the meeting they asked me if
I'd feel more comfortable talking to someone
Who isn't plus size because of my issues surrounding
Eating and body image.
I said not at all.

And then somewhere in the midst they say,
"I am what you fear."
I felt so bad.
I asked them if they were comfortable with me discussing my body
image and other related issues and they said that there would be a lot
for me to do to make them uncomfortable. But for some reason, I
don't feel like they should have asked if I was uncomfortable with
them nor "I am what you fear" — is this appropriate to say to a
client?

A week later they push our meeting back a day — the day turns
into another week.

After that week I try to reschedule and I don't hear from them.
I probably insulted them and that was not my intention.
They must not like me.
I am what you fear.
It replays in me like a threaded needle piercing thick corduroy.

They respond. I don't.
The school calls
But I don't answer.

I'm too embarrassed to go back.
I'd rather bite my tongue
Than spit out my hurt
To a stranger
That has no desire
To even help
The stereotypical sorority girl.

I Listen, I Read, I Cave.

I've never spoken a word.
Everyone around me,
Filled with energetic emotions,
Fueling what they talk about.
They're loud
But they don't speak.
They talk over me,
Tumbling and stumbling
Through selfish sentences.
I listen.

I read, I cave.
I've never written my story.
Everyone around me,
Filled with pretentious smarts,
Fueling their misspelled jargon.
Their pens don't stop moving
But they aren't writing.
They scribble over my truths I
Have yet to write.
I read.

I cave.
I never grew to be bamboo.
Everyone around me,
Sprouting to become weeds,
Fueling their infectious nature.
Their presence is massive and strong
And they tower over my little stem,
Weakening at the root, struggling to
Rise amongst the weeds
Surrounding me.

The Mind of an Artist

Art being transferred
To the back of my wrist
With just the sweeping of
A paint brush against my
Blank canvas.
Primer paint.
The mind of an artist.

The endless ecstasy
That's given to me
As I allow my fingers
To descend down
The greasy bottle
That connects my
Gut to my mouth.
Once I reach the
Bottom of the bottle,
Liquid abruptly brings
Beautiful kaleidoscopes
Into a circular canvas.
Oil paint.
The mind of an artist.

But then I think of the cacophonous
sound of silence that surrounds me.
The mind of an artist.

The imaging of little beads
In opulent orange buckets
Eradicated by the top of
My paint bottle. Smoothly swallowed.
Textured paint.

The mind of an artist.

The sweet dream of letting
Red paint stream its way
Off my arm and submerge
Itself into water.
Watercolor paint.
The mind of an artist.
The euphonic sound of a
Squirt gun imprinting
My skull with colorful paint.
Splatter paint.
The mind of an artist.

Paint ignites the fire.
Burns way any miserable thought
And warms the expression of creation.
The mind of an artist.

For I remind myself
Paint is subjective.
The mind of an artist.

No one can see the paint
I have stored in my cabinets.
The mind of an artist.

If anyone were to open
My cabinets and find my paint,
Would they find my canvas
Abandoned and blank?

Pinned

He was drunk and sad.
He put his head
On my shoulder.
I let him confide in me.
I pat his head.
He lowered himself.
Head on my lap.
Like a little kid.
I think it's odd.
But I don't mind.
Until his hands circle
My thighs and peck me.
I think it's weird
But maybe some of my friends
Are just more affectionate.

He shuts the lights
And slowly pushes
Me down and climbs
On top of me.
I have no idea
What he is doing.
We're just friends.
We've always been
Just friends.
I'm confused.
He comes closer
To me.
I've never had
Someone's lips
Leave an imprint

On my neck
Until now.
I want to get him off
Of me but I don't know
How he's going to respond.
"What about Ally?"
I blurt out.
He's lost.
There never really was
Another girl, was there?
He only ever wanted
To deceive me.
I tell myself it's not so bad
I just want to go home.
I wish someone could
Call me and say they need
Me right now.

His hands around my throat.
His hands all over my body.
I told him I don't want that.
I told him to stop.
I told him he shouldn't.
I told him I want to go home.
He wouldn't let me leave.
He begged and pleaded.
I didn't want his hands on
My throat again.
What if he did something worse?
Maybe if I'm complacent
It won't be so bad.

I couldn't sleep
As he touched places
That are sacred to me

I kept telling myself
It's not so bad, it's life experience.

The life experience
Of walking home in clothes
You loved and now see
As different shades of
Disgust as if it was its own
Separate color
You throw them
Into your dirty hamper
Because the clothes
You slept in felt
Dirty on your body
The clothes may have
Been cleaner than your body
You scorch yourself in the shower
Early in the morning
Trying to scrub his
Hand prints off of your
Chest
Thighs
Hair
Backside
Neck

No matter how hard
You scrub, the soap
And water are just
Not enough
To fix what's been
Made to feel unclean

You cry because you
Weren't raped.

You cry because it
Felt like you were going to be.

Your girlhood is still
Intact but he tried
To selfishly claim it.
He knew you've never
Been held before
And he soured the
Sweetness of intimacy
You craved for with
Your person.

After you dry
Your body off
You feel his calloused
Hands wrapped around
Your throat.
It could have been worse
And it wasn't.
He didn't go further.
Thank goodness he was tired
And fell asleep.

You lay in your bed staring at the
Rising sun peeking through your
Open window wondering what
All of this meant and what happened

But he messages you.
No apology.
No check-in. But a:
"Don't tell Ally about last night."

You wouldn't want anyone to know

About last night, why would you
Want to be painted as a whore
When you could paint the night as
Non-existent?

You come home for Thanksgiving
And your family asks what
The small, purple mark on your neck is.
You say you don't know with a crack of a smile.

Ally messages you
Asking about your once
Mutual friend but more
Than a friend for Ally.

You tell her he's not into her
And she can find someone
That truly likes her.

She keeps asking
More and more drunken
Questions over misspelled messages
And that's when you tell her
He tried to get with you.
She gets angry.
You coddle her using words
Like cuddling and just platonic things
But that wasn't truthful.
Either way she didn't care
What happened to you
With the context clues you
Hope she'd comprehend
But her drunken illiteracy
Let her end up dating him.

When they broke up
You felt obligated to
Be nice to him.
To still befriend him.
He listened to you
You listened to him
He never tried to
Touch you again
But when you brought
Up what happened to you
He said that it didn't matter
Because he was drunk.

Ally drunkenly messages
You that she has a problem with you
Because of what you did with him.

Friends bring up what Ally told them.
You say, "It wasn't like that."
You cry to them and that's when
You're honest.
Even though you try
To believe what he said
"It didn't matter because he was drunk."

You try to defend him
Because you think
You made meaning
Out of really nothing.
He didn't rape you.
But he does call you stupid.
But he does lie to you.

You can't take it anymore
And eventually you are brave

Enough to release him
Even though he pinned you down.

You have a nightmare
About him and that
Haunting night
Your Mom sees you crying
And asks what's wrong?

And that's when you're honest.

It did matter.

Hippocampus

Results

Dr. Old Man called me.
Blood test came back
With great results
But no answers
As to why I am
Feeling so sad
numb
dark
Weak.
My blood is healthy
But my mind is not.

I want to get better.
But how can I
Teach myself
After a millennia
Of neglecting
My body?

"We're Here For You"

"Hi Kayla, from the online sheet you filled out, it looks like you'd benefit from more specialized therapy. We are only general counseling. I'll send you some places to look into."

-Said the place that also has specialized therapy options available

"Sorry Kayla, unfortunately we do not accept your insurance. We do have out-of-network benefits."

-$500 a week for the **BEST** help a person in crisis can buy!

"Sorry Kayla, unfortunately we do not accept your insurance. We do have out-of-network benefits. It will be out of pocket so we recommend finding a place that takes your insurance."

-$300 out of pocket for DBT

"Text a therapist today for only $65 a session."

-A fucking social media ad

"Estrogen levels are extremely low. Let's put you on birth control."

-The day I started birth control in high school was the day I truly hated my body

"Did you try talking to a counselor on campus? It's completely free."

-Professors

"I am what you fear."

-College Counselor that canceled after one session

In high school I went to psychotherapy and she took my insurance. But I don't need psychotherapy. I need something more "specialized."

Frontal

Privilege of Peace

Where are the men in Baghdad?
>   I walked through the door and saw you again.
The women and children and animals are all there, right?
>   It was the end of February when you would shoot your
>   stars at me.
The poverty is there, the massacres are there?
>   I've never seen shooting stars as bright and as big as yours.
But no men?
>   You were iridescent—
The women walk the dilapidated streets, with their babes on their
hips?
>   —A nocturnal commodity of luminescence my universe
>   moved toward.
The children hide in torn towers terrified of troops?
>   My heart for a moment in time was forever frozen for you.
The cacophony of a single bullet entering the heart of an innocent?
>   You blink and suddenly your sparkle is depleted.
But where are the men in Baghdad?
>   Your universe walked past me and I hoped we would
>   collide.
These innocents need help?
>   We never did.
Help.

>   When did you stop seeing my stars?
Fearful of freedom, they flee from the unfathomable fight.
>   My stars shoot at you.
Souls, searching so desperately for peace.
>   You've never seen my shooting stars?
The innocents leave behind the world they once loved.
>   You leave behind the illusion of collision.

They now bear witness to a new world.

>Our world would wash away the watery worries we wish to withdraw from.

These refugees cling to a piece of peace.

>You understand but you left the idea behind you and above your skies.

They force themselves to fall in love with the names "Jane" and "John."

>You can't force yourself to pull down your skies for me.

Teach themselves "Hello, how are you?"

>I learn I cannot catch your shooting stars.

People pity their broken plosives.

>I pity the words you haven't said to me.

Where are the men in Baghdad?

>Where are you?

Still obsessed with the absence of peace?

>My mind is a waterfall recycling our small moments over and over.

Still maliciously murdering mothers?

>I resist at first but I soon flee from the never-ending cycle of waterworks.

The men in Baghdad don't exist, only malevolence.

>You don't exist, only memories.

The refugees are courageous as they tread their way to American soil, they've been through so much.

>My heart only aches. A privileged turmoil that slowly clouds my progressive speech.

Refugees from Baghdad relied relentlessly on peace to get them through.

>I wanted peace but not with the memories of you.

11/22

11/22
I thought I knew you
Enough to be with
You no matter what.

11:22
I'd text you
But you'd be sleeping.
Good night.

1122
I see you
And use this as my sign
To call but you don't want to.

11
Times I asked you
To call me when you could
And somehow you didn't
Instead you told me
"The phone works both ways."

22
Quiet hours without you
Pass me by and I am
Detached from you — I feel
Great, no longer longing for
The you I thought I knew on
11/22.

Tumor[7]

Malevolent mastermind
Makes morals a malignancy.
Someone so charming and benign
At first changed his consistency.

Damaged deceiver dependent
On getting what he wants:
Cajoling and coaxing independent
Individuals and with their hearts he taunts.

Calling, crying, characterizing
These women with his wounds.
Wishing to wash away, empathizing
With his terrorizing, tumultuous tunes.

Little lies longing
A less-lasting love in lives.
Used in a malicious manipulating
Game where his hurt ego thrives.

Naive. Not knowing
His heinous intentions
Are secretly sewing
Women's insecure interventions.

After he finishes using
His objects, he gains their constancy
And leaves. They see each other and his abusing
Ways, wiring feelings of envy and jealousy.

Left lonesome and lied to.

Still struck by his charm and humor,
Unable to understand the utopic man who
Is not a man at all, but a tight tumor
Around their hearts and minds,
Slowly suffocating each of them
And sometimes he grinds
Against their hearts, killing one of a kind gems.

Ghost in a Box

I breathe and I breathe
And I breathe until I can
No longer fathom living
In a box, designed for freedom
But adapted to create confinement.

I run and cry and kneel
Before porcelain. My tears
Fall onto my fingers while
They fidget in my mouth.

My ears ring with cries
And my mouth opens wide,
Releasing everything (not much)
I consumed.

I stop and cry to myself.
No one can hear me.
No one can see me.
No one can touch me.
I am a ghost.

I just hope, at this
Time, even if I'm
Half-alive,
Someone
Will hear me.

She Is a Poppy Seed

She is a poppy seed
Stuck in between your teeth.

You don't remove your teeth
To keep the discomfort
Of the poppy seed, right?

NO, you cleanse your worth and
Swish and swish until she
Spills into the sink. You
Wash her away because
She never gave value
To your life. She is a

Poppy seed, remember.

Just a Girl

I'M A GIRL
AND I WALK MYSELF
THROUGH THE SNOWY
WHITE ROADS WHERE
CARS CAN'T SEE ME
I AM INVINCIBLE!

im just a girl.
i walk by myself —
dark alleyways,
street lights surrender:
the headlights of cars —
nearly hitting me,
i'm too invisible:
but i stand in bright red —
a protective coat,
keeping shelter:

am i just a girl?

Slaughter Home

It's the sliver of flesh
Carved out of body
Made to mock
The cows.
I don't want
To be the cows.
They want to be me

But my arms

Leather
Leather
Leather.

Wrinkly
Pruny
Dry.

Dead is not a texture.

It's the crush of small tubes
In hands of ignorance
Greedy for profit
Over secretion
Meant for the cows.
I don't want to be the cows.
They want to be me

But my stomach acid

Milk

Milk
Milk.

Thick
Chunky
Sour.

Dead is not a taste.

It's the botched pieces
Of tongues chopped
To shut up the cows.
I don't want
To be the cows.
They want to be me

But my voice

Aphasia
Aphasia
Aphasia.

Dead is not in my voice

But it rings a bell
To my night terrors.

The cows want to be me
But they don't know
I feel just like them

But no one to blame
Other than myself.

Viral

I wallow in your words.
You're a pitiful muse,
Mounded by dirt, making mountains
Out of the mole hills you
Trapped me in.

I swallow your words
And break them down into
Bite-size pieces, they don't sit
In my gut right. I give them
Back to you. Only this time,
They're no longer sweet and sugary
But bitter and acidic. Your
Words burn
My throat.
Little polyps on the tips of
My knuckles,
Teeth marks on
My two fingers,
Your words trigger
My body.
I'd purge in a giftbox
And tie a pretty
Ribbon on top just to
Respectfully return your words
But they run a fever in me.
Your words are a virus, not
An antidote.
I may be ill
But you are the sick one.

Slip

My heart,
         My eyes,
                  My ears,
                           My nose

         Feel the pain that comes and goes.

                                    My mind,
                                 My face,
                           My arms,
                        My mouth,

         Forget all we were about.

My time,
         My place,
                  My future,
                     My life

            On this Earth will remind me

                                    Of when
                              I will
                           Not hurt
                        No more.

            The steps I am taking in

My life
         Are what
                  Keep me

Sane yet

I descend, I fall down but

All ways

I get

Back up

But it's

Difficult to be strong

When you

Hurt me.

I hate

You but

I love you and I want to help

You but

You're too

Far gone

For me

To help you try to not slip

To space,

To sea,

To stars

To dust.

You're escalating down life.

Did you

Love me?

Did you

Love us?

Your heartbeat is speeding up.

Do you
        Need help?
                Are you
                        Dead or

Are you trying a new high?

That is
Not love
That'll be
Your death.
You slipped
And I
Cried so
Much be-
Cause I
Loved you
So much.
My steps
Of life
I climb
Each day
Be cause
I don't
Want to
Slip like
You did.
Slip 'way
From tough
Times by
Reading,
Singing,
Dancing,

Painting
But you're
Set in
Your ways.
This won't
Be me.
I won't
Slip be-
Cause I
Have learned
From your
Mistakes.

Broken Barbie[8,9]

Confined in a
Plastic box, where
My vision is impaired
By the rose-colored film
That hangs in front of
My painted eyes.
But I'm beautiful.

My hollow body:
Standard and recognizable
Freezes. I don't move.
But I'm still beautiful.

He comes around
The corner and stares.
His gaze has me inaudible.
I just stand there.
He smiles and comes closer.
He looks beautiful through my film.

He reaches out his hand
To me but I can't grab it.
He picks me up—
Ready to rescue me from confinement.
He takes me out of my box
And holds me. I've never been held.
Being wrapped in his hands
Feels beautiful.

He shifts his gaze.
His eyes are stuck.

But he moves, holding me with one
Hand. While his left picks up
Another me. Am I still beautiful?

My smile is her smile.
My body is her body.
Maybe she's more blonde than I?
Her outfit much more tacky than
Mine. He holds her and
Looks at her the way he did
With me. Am I beautiful?

His smile now breaks my smile.
He puts me back in my box—
Where the film is tarnished
And my eyes melt down
The rest of my polished face.
He takes her — in her box and all.
She is deemed more beautiful.

I'm left limp
While he walks down the aisle
With her. Why her?
With all of my numbed pain.
My box falls on the tile.
My rose-colored film is no longer.
My hair is frazzled.
My body broken into pieces.
My eyes blinded by harsh
Fluorescent light and my smile gone.
I'm not beautiful.

Bucket of Rice

The bucket of rice is empty.
But you said you filled it.
You can't fill a bucket with your void
When the bucket is meant to hold rice.
Your insecurities and your worries
Don't belong in a bucket
That can pour out and drench
My clothes, my face, my hair, my body,
My whole being.
Beings are not buckets.
Can I cook your worries?
Can I season your fears?
I can weigh myself down with these, sure.
But that's not what a bucket is meant to do
To me.
Weigh me down.

Judgement Day

Is every day.
Even when I kiss
Your face with a warm
Breeze in tropical weather,
I see how you cover yourself
From my sunshine. You scorn my light.

I could create a hurricane that leaves
You ripped and torn into tiny little pieces,
Your skin pierced and your reputation bruised in
An exhaustingly humid threshold no one can stand.

And if you flee I will find you
Hidden amongst snowy white mountains
And haunt you with my alluring eyes and
My lupine grin. I will flash my fangs for fun
While you replicate humidity within your body.

I am not afraid of you.
When you think of me
I am there, mocking your malevolency,
Standing and staring at shards of shells
Shot and aimed for me but severely missed.

So stay where you are.
Squirm in my sunshine
Sweat in my heatwaves.
Pick at the flesh you so proudly wore
Around me and all the others you hurt.

I won't hurt you the way you hurt me.

I am not you.
I don't need to hurt you but I can.

So sit back, recline your lounge chair
And sip your whiskey with unease.
Your umbrella should never have said
I am too much.
I am the sun
And you were simply never enough.

The roller coaster takes me back inside, but this time it moves slowly, it shuts my bedroom door gently and opens the blinds. There's a glimmer of daylight in my room. I can see my bedroom, I can see myself. My wrists and my thighs are sore and pink. The roller coaster moves unnecessarily slow, slow enough to put on a jacket and pants to cover the sunshine I attempted to make for myself. I wonder if the sunshine I attempted to make for myself is the reason why the roller coaster is moving so slowly. Is the roller coaster about to stop? I don't want it to stop. The roller coaster has never fully stopped before. Am I stopping the roller coaster right now? Am I about to? I really don't want it to stop. I can't believe the roller coaster is about to stop. What do I do? I can't ask anyone how to get the roller coaster to function normally again because then they'll see the way that I hijacked it with my selfish attempt to create sunshine in the dark for myself. Where are the lights in my room? It's too dark outside to use daylight. What can I do? Can I even fix the roller coaster by myself? And just like that the roller coaster busts through the window and spirals towards the gray clouds. I used to love going up but now I look forward to going down. I broke the roller coaster.

Notes

1. "The Interrogation Room" is in conversation with T. S. Elliot's "The Love Song of J. Alfred Prufrock." Some excerpts, such as "a patient etherized upon a table," "So how should I presume," and "In the room women come and go / Talking of Michelangelo," are direct quotes from Elliot's work. "The Love Song of J. Alfred Prufrock," first published in *Poetry* magazine in 1915, is in the public domain.

2. "Toys Made for the Girl and Boy That Play" was originally published in the July 2021 edition of *Modern Renaissance* magazine.

3. "Lizard" references fourteen songs by The Doors: "Break on Through (To the Other Side)," "Love Her Madly," "Tell All the People," "Touch Me," "End of the Night," "Celebration of the Lizard," "Light My Fire," "L.A. Woman," "Hyacinth House," "Hello, I Love You," "Queen of the Highway," "When the Music's Over," "The Unknown Soldier," and "We Could Be So Good Together." As of this book's date of publication, rights to The Doors' catalogue are owned by Primary Wave Music.

4. This final quote is from Greta Van Fleet's "Light My Love," written by Greg Kurstin, Daniel Wagner, Joshua Kiszka, Justin Kiszka, and Samuel Kiszka.

5. "To disappear" is in conversation with William Shakespeare's *Macbeth*. As part of Shakespeare's 1623 *First Folio*, *Macbeth* is in the public domain.

6. This quote is from Shakespeare's *Macbeth*.

7. "Tumor" was previously published in the Fall 2020 edition of *The Great Lake Review* and the July 2021 edition of *Modern Renaissance* magazine.

8. Barbie is a trademark of Mattel, Inc.

9. "Broken Barbie" was originally published in the July 2021 edition of *Modern Renaissance*.

Author's Progress Note

A journal entry from March 3, 2021:

Dreams can come true if you free them from your imaginative desires and allow the universe to acknowledge what you deserve.

A journal entry from March 17, 2021:

Do you ever see everything that's wrong with the world?

All I want is to save this world but how can one woman save this world by herself?

I don't have control over our world but I can control the world with which I surround myself. I can control the world within my mind, therefore I can control my contributions to the world surrounding me.

A journal entry from April 21, 2023:

After so many months of thinking I've lost you, I finally found you.

These writings and journal entries are powerful and may seem dark, if read only once. They may have spoken for you when you didn't know how to ask others for help or when you were isolated by your mind. Please, always remember that these feelings and harmful thoughts do not make you a monster. These make you a human.

You'll be so proud to know that many of your contents are being published! You have worked so hard, felt so much, and now every tribulation written has led to this beautiful and rewarding moment.

You may not have been able to get the help you need mentally BUT you were recently diagnosed with an autoimmune disease that explains why you have felt the way you have for so long. This diagnosis is a blessing because it explains part of your sadness, tiredness, and mood swings. I am so happy for you and I hope you are, too.

From 2019-2022, a whirlwind of emotions and experiences emerged into all that shaped me into the person we are today. You, journal, are a reflection of who I was and will always be a part of who I am. I can tell past versions of myself that reflect within you, it truly does get better. You were never perfect and I am still not perfect (even though we always try to be). I don't need to be perfect today because I am in love with my life. Sure there are some days that remind me of you, where I feel so deeply and dark. These days can never measure up to the pure gratitude and resilience we have been gifted.

Acknowledgements

First and foremost, I'd like to extend my gratitude to Gina. Thank you so much for your time, effort, and most importantly, your kindness. Words cannot describe how thankful I am to have met you when I did. I am so lucky to have an editor and a publisher that is passionate about what they do and is so easy to talk to. You made a dream of mine come true. I hope you truly know how grateful I am to work with you.

I'd like to extend my gratitude to Gina's business partner, Sam. Your bubbly energy and financing skills have been such a treat! I am grateful you are a part of this process (and not just because I can't do math to save my life). Thank you for all of your hard work.

Next, I'd like to thank my mom. My mom has kept each and every one of my stories I wrote since kindergarten. To say my mom is my biggest fan is an understatement! She does so much for me (almost everything if I'm being honest). She is my best friend, my confidante, and my biggest advocate. For all of my rheumatology appointments, flare-ups, bad days — she's there for them all. She can make a bad day better with just a simple call. She's the reason why I am where I am today. I am honored to be her daughter.

Papa! My greatest stories stem from you. You are one of the people I admire most in my life. You came to my first poetry reading and bought a copy of the anthology my piece was in, just so I could sign it for you. You are one of my greatest supporters and I hope I make you proud. And just remember, how many of your other grandkids dedicated a book to you? Guess my title of favorite grandchild still stands (sorry Laci)!

Dad and Joey! Elfinator and Water Boy. Thank you guys for dealing with me and supporting my work. It's a great feeling when I join in on a conversation and my brother is already promoting my book to everyone in the room. Each day after work I come home to these two and they always want updates on the book. I may not say it often, but thank you.

To my family, friends, and coworkers. Thank you for your unwavering support. Shoutout to Gianna for looking over the legal components for me! Aunt Donna, I remember you told me that you used to write poetry in high school. I hope you write again soon.

To my professors and mentors from Oswego, thank you so much for encouraging me to keep writing and to trust the process of life.

Prescriptions

A list of habits, books, websites, and social media pages that helped me heal and continue to heal. I hope you try some of these out!

Habits
- Read a book outside (if the weather is good)
- Think of three people/things you are grateful for when you wake up
- Move your body (dance, go to the gym, walk, etc.)
- Take your vitamins!
- Take cold showers
- Go to the beach once a month
- Take pictures of what makes you smile
- Smile at your reflection
- Drink water
- Get matcha with friends
- Give compliments to strangers
- Write out affirmations nine times each
- Put effort into your appearance (style your hair, do your makeup, etc.)
- Clean your room
- Talk outwardly to the universe
- Scream your favorite song lyrics in your car
- Journal, and let out everything you've been holding in
- Meditate (or even playing meditation music before you sleep helps, too)
- Go out on an adventure with friends or family outside of your hometown
- Delete all social media apps for a day

- Create art

Personal Growth Books
- *Daring Greatly* by Brene Brown
- *The Defining Decade* by Dr. Meg Jay
- *The Four Agreements* by Don Miguel Ruiz
- *Heal Your Body* by Louise Hay
- *Healing the Hurt Within* by Jan Sutton
- *In Search of Wisdom* by Joyce Meyer
- *You are a Badass* by Jen Sincero

Websites
- www.attachment.personaldevelopmentschool.com
- www.5lovelanguages.com
- www.self-compassion.org
- www.nationaleatingdisorders.org
- www.familyhconline.com
- www.16personalities.com
- www.myhumandesign.com
- www.cafeastrology.com

Instagram Pages
- @sistercody
- @thirdeyekingdom
- @vegan.f.t.a
- @gabe_weiss
- @christineowensart
- @hummus.bean

TikTok Pages
- @yourhealingbuddy
- @drewafualo

- @pitbull
- @hunterprosper
- @maliaschmalleger
- @spencewuah
- @bobbykazz

About the Author

Kayla Estelle Elfers is a poet and writer from Long Island, NY. Her poetry has been published in Bards Annual: A Poetry Anthology, The Great Lake Review, The Oswegonian Newspaper, and Modern Renaissance magazine by Culturally. Kayla holds a degree in creative writing from the State University of New York at Oswego and is a graduate student at St. Joseph's University, New York.

Printed in the USA
CPSIA information can be obtained
at www.ICGtesting.com
LVHW040814131023
760664LV00009B/737